Second Edition

Beyond Birdies

A Parent's Guide to Help Your Child Win at Golf & Life

Joseph DiChiara
PGA Professional

979-8-9941422-2-6

979-8-9941422-3-3

First Edition: 2025

Second Edition: 2026

Cover design & Interior design by: RH Publishing

Printed in the United States of America

CONTENTS

Chapter 1

How Children Really Learn Golf

THE FIRST TEE AT a junior tournament is a strange place.

It's quiet, but not calm. Parents gather a few steps back, careful not to interfere, yet unable to fully step away. Sunglasses hide eyes that are already scanning posture, tempo, and confidence. Kids shuffle their feet, roll putts that don't count, take practice swings that suddenly feel heavier than they did five minutes ago.

Nothing has gone wrong yet.

And still, everyone feels it.

Parents often describe moments like this later when they say, "I just knew it wasn't going to be their day." Not because of anything they saw technically, but because something felt different. The body language was off.

The energy was tight. The ease that showed up on the range didn't follow them to the tee.

By the time the round ends and the clubs are back in the trunk, the same question surfaces almost every time.

"We practice so much. Why doesn't it show up?"

It's a fair question. An honest one. And it almost always comes from care, not pressure. But hidden inside it is an assumption that quietly shapes the junior golf experience more than most parents realize: the belief that learning should look logical from the outside.

For children, learning rarely looks that way.

Most kids begin golf exactly as they should.

They swing freely. They chase distance. They try shots that make no sense strategically but feel exciting. They miss badly and laugh. They learn without realizing they're learning because there is no fear attached to the outcome.

Golf, at this stage, is play.

Then something subtle changes.

It might be the first tournament.

It might be a comment from another parent.

It might be a lesson that suddenly feels serious.

It might be the realization that scores are being noticed.

Without anyone intending it, golf shifts from something to explore into something to perform.

That's usually when adults start talking more.

Feedback increases. Corrections arrive faster. Explanations fill the space between swings. Parents and coaches want to help, to guide, to support improvement. And in doing so, the game slowly moves out of the body and into the mind.

This is where learning begins to change.

Children do not learn movement the way adults learn information.

Adults assume understanding comes first. If a child knows what went wrong, the fix should follow. That logic works for school assignments and test prep. It does not work the same way for movement.

Movement lives in a different part of the brain.

When a child swings a golf club, their brain is

coordinating balance, timing, vision, feel, and emotion all at once. This happens below conscious thought. It's instinctive. It's adaptive. And it requires freedom.

When adults interrupt that process too often with explanation or correction, the brain responds predictably, it protects itself.

Protection looks like hesitation.

It looks like stiffness.

It looks like confusion where confidence used to live.

Parents often describe this as a loss of confidence. What's really happening is a loss of trust, in the body, in feel, in instinct.

The child hasn't forgotten how to swing. They've stopped trusting themselves to do it.

This is why learning in junior golf so often looks messy.

Children frequently get worse before they get better. Scores rise unexpectedly. Mechanics appear unstable. Confidence flickers without warning. Just when things seem to be coming together, everything falls apart.

From the outside, this feels like regression.

From the inside, the brain is reorganizing.

The brain does not improve in straight lines. It improves in waves. Old patterns loosen before new ones stabilize. Coordination reshuffles as bodies grow and change. When adults rush to "fix" these unstable phases, learning stalls.

Good intentions can quietly slow progress.

This is one of the hardest truths for parents to accept, because it asks them to tolerate discomfort without intervening.

I once worked with a young player who looked exceptional on the range.

The contact was solid. The tempo was smooth. Confidence radiated from every swing. Parents whispered about how ready they looked.

By the third hole of the tournament, everything unraveled.

The swing tightened. Misses grew larger. The child kept looking back after shots, not for instruction, but reassurance. Not for answers, but safety.

After the round, the parent said, "They know how to do

this. Why can't they do it when it matters?"

The parent's question revealed their value of performance and results over learning golf's deeper lessons.

Knowing had replaced trusting.

The range felt safe. The course felt evaluative. One environment allowed exploration. The other triggered protection. The child didn't fail, they adapted to pressure.

This pattern repeats itself endlessly in junior golf, and it has nothing to do with talent.

Most parents believe they're helping when they give technical advice. Often, the advice itself is correct.

The problem is timing.

Children's bodies are changing constantly. Growth alters balance. Strength arrives before coordination, or coordination before strength. What felt natural last season can suddenly feel impossible. When we layer heavy technical thinking onto a moving target, children lose trust in their own feel.

They stop swinging freely.

They start monitoring themselves.

And once a child begins monitoring movement instead of trusting it, performance becomes unpredictable, especially under pressure.

This isn't a motivation issue.

It isn't a discipline issue.

It's a developmental one.

Children don't need early mastery. They need space.

Parents often underestimate how much children absorb without words.

Kids feel tension before it's spoken. They sense disappointment even when adults try to hide it. A sigh after a missed putt can carry more weight than an entire lesson. Silence in the car can feel louder than criticism.

Over time, these moments shape how children experience the game.

Some become perfectionists, afraid to swing freely.

Some withdraw, protecting themselves emotionally.

Some lose joy altogether, even if results improve.

The children who thrive long-term aren't the ones shielded from difficulty. They're the ones allowed to experience difficulty without fear of losing approval.

This is where the parent's role becomes most important, not as a coach, but as a stabilizer.

Time for Reflection

Pause here before reading on.

Think back to your child's last three tournaments or rounds. Not the scores, the moments around them. The walk to the first tee. The reaction after a missed shot. The drive home.

Ask yourself honestly:

When my child struggled, what was harder for me—their learning process, or my discomfort watching it? There is no right answer. Only awareness.

On the next page, take some time to write about your internal experience when your child is struggling. What do you want to say to them? What do you hold back? What emotions show up first?

Taking this time to reflect on how tournaments have

gone in the past is not about changing your behavior yet. It's about understanding how your child feels in the environment.

Confidence does not come from success.

It comes from safety.

Children who feel safe to struggle eventually learn to succeed. Children who feel pressure to perform often lose joy long before skill catches up.

Safety doesn't mean lowering standards. It means separating performance from approval. It means allowing golf to teach them lessons without attaching fear to the learning process.

Parents shape this more than anyone else in a child's golf life.

Not through instruction.

Through presence.

A Commitment Worth Making

Before the next practice stretch or tournament, consider making a quiet commitment to yourself.

For the next few weeks, commits to letting the mistakes belong to the game, not the relationship.

This might mean fewer words.

It might mean a calmer tone.

It might mean letting a bad round end without a discussion of what went wrong.

On the next page, write one sentence you hope your child remembers about golf ten years from now. Not about winning. Not about trophies.

What do you want them to remember about how it felt to play while you were watching?

Sign and date it.

That sentence will guide you better than any swing thought ever could.

Golf will challenge your child in ways few sports can. It will test patience, confidence, and identity. Those challenges are unavoidable.

But you can help them avoid attaching fear to their learning process.

Children don't need parents who know everything

about golf.

They need parents who protect curiosity long enough for skill to grow.

When learning feels safe, improvement follows.

Not immediately.

Not predictably.

But honestly, and for life.

Chapter 2

Your Child's Unique Development Journey

At some point, almost every parent asks the same quiet question.

It usually comes after a tournament, not during it. After the adrenaline fades. After the comparisons settle in.

"Why does it seem like everyone else is improving faster?"

Sometimes the question is about distance. Sometimes it's about scores. Sometimes it's about confidence. And sometimes it's about another child, one who practices less, complains more, or seems less invested, yet somehow keeps performing better.

This is the moment when doubt begins to creep in.

Not doubt about your child's effort.

Doubt about the path.

What most parents don't realize is that this question isn't really about golf. It's about development. And development is never fair, linear, or predictable, especially in children.

Every junior golfer is on a timeline that cannot be rushed.

Some children grow early. Their bodies get strong quickly. The ball starts flying farther. Scores drop fast. Adults notice. Praise increases. Expectations rise.

Other children develop quietly. Coordination comes before power. Feel comes before speed. They look average, until they don't.

Both paths are normal. Both paths are temporary.

The problem begins when adults mistake timing for talent.

Early success feels reassuring. Late development feels uncomfortable. And because parents naturally want certainty, they often assume that what shows up first must be better.

Golf doesn't work that way.

I once coached two players the same age, practicing at the same facility, competing in the same events.

One hit the ball a mile. The other struggled to keep up. Parents whispered. Comparisons were unavoidable.

Five years later, their paths had crossed completely.

The early bloomer hit a plateau. The game felt heavy. Expectations were high, but adaptability was low. The late developer had learned how to adjust, how to solve problems, how to stay patient. When physical development caught up, the skill foundation was already there.

Nothing had gone wrong.

Development had simply unfolded on different schedules.

Children are not just growing physically. They're growing neurologically, emotionally, and socially, all at once.

Some kids can handle pressure early. Others internalize it deeply. Some thrive on competition. Others need time to build confidence before results appear. None of these traits are permanent. They change as children mature.

This is why comparing children at young ages is so misleading.

You are rarely comparing skill to skill.

You are comparing timelines.

Parents who understand this stop chasing fixes and start protecting progress. They recognize that today's struggles are not forecasts, they're snapshots.

Golf careers are not built in snapshots. They're built over years.

One of the most dangerous moments in junior golf happens when adults panic during natural developmental transitions.

Growth spurts disrupt balance. New strength changes timing. Confidence wavers as identity shifts. What once felt automatic suddenly feels foreign.

Parents often respond by adding more structure, more explanation, more correction. They assume the child is regressing.

In reality, the body is recalibrating.

Children don't need more information during these phases. They need reassurance. They need permission to feel awkward. They need adults who don't interpret temporary instability as permanent failure.

When adults stay calm, children adapt faster.

Another quiet truth parents rarely hear is this:

Children experience golf differently depending on who they believe they are.

Some children identify early as "the good golfer." When results dip, they feel like they're losing themselves. Others see golf as something they do, not who they are. Their confidence bends but doesn't break.

Parents influence this more than they realize.

When praise is tied to outcomes, identity narrows. When encouragement is tied to effort, curiosity, and resilience, identity expands.

The goal isn't to remove ambition. It's to prevent golf from becoming the only place a child feels valued.

Time for Reflection

Pause here.

Think about how you describe your child to others. Not

just their golf, who they are.

Do you lead with scores? Rankings? Wins?

Or do you talk about curiosity, work ethic, creativity, or resilience?

Now think about how your child hears those descriptions.

On the next page, write a few sentences about how you believe your child currently sees themselves in golf. Strong. Behind. Confident. Pressured. Unsure.

This isn't about labeling them correctly. It's about understanding how they feel about their golf experience.

Children don't all peak at the same time. Some peak early and struggle to adapt. Others struggle early and build durability. Neither path guarantees anything.

What matters most is whether the environment allows growth to continue.

Parents who trust the process stay focused on development, not comparison. They understand that patience isn't passive, it's protective.

I've seen countless players who looked "behind" for

years suddenly surge forward when timing aligned. I've also seen players who dominated early burn out under pressure they didn't yet have the tools to manage.

The difference was rarely talent.

It was environment.

Children grow best when adults allow skill building and development to unfold naturally instead of forcing them to practice to improve performance.

A Commitment Worth Making

Before the next season or tournament stretch, make a quiet agreement.

Commit to stop comparing your child's progress to others and start paying attention to their growth over time.

On the next page, write down three ways your child has grown in the past year that have nothing to do with scores or rankings.

Sign and date it.

This commitment doesn't lower expectations. It redirects them.

Every junior golfer's journey is unique.

Some paths look smooth. Others look messy. Both can lead somewhere meaningful if adults resist the urge to rush.

Your child does not need to be ahead.

They need to be supported.

When parents trust that their child will develop and sharpen skills according to their own unique timeline, children learn to trust themselves.

And that trust is what lasts.

Chapter 3

Creating the Right Environment

Children don't learn golf in isolation.

They learn it inside environments, quiet ones and loud ones, supportive ones and stressful ones, intentional ones and accidental ones. Most parents think of environment as practice time, coaching quality, or tournament schedule. In reality, the most powerful environment in junior golf is emotional.

It's the feeling a child carries onto the first tee.

It's the tone of the car ride home.

It's the reaction they expect after a missed putt.

Those moments shape learning more than any drill ever could.

Parents rarely set out to create a stressful environment. It forms slowly, built on good intentions, expectations, comparisons, and the natural desire to help. Over time, the environment around golf begins to carry weight, tension builds gradually without anyone noticing.

I've seen two children with nearly identical skill sets experience golf in completely different ways.

One plays freely, recovers quickly from mistakes, and enjoys the challenge even on difficult days. The other plays cautiously, fears mistakes, and spirals when things don't go well.

The difference is rarely coaching.

It's environment.

One child feels safe to explore. The other feels responsible for results.

Safety doesn't mean comfort. It means emotional stability. It means mistakes don't threaten belonging. It means golf outcomes don't leak into relationships.

Children sense this instinctively. They know when approval feels conditional, even if no one says it out loud.

The environment begins long before the first swing.

It starts in conversations during the week. In how practice is framed. In whether golf feels like something they *get* to do or something they *have* to do. It lives in subtle comments about other players, rankings, or expectations.

It lives in silence, too.

A quiet car ride can feel supportive or heavy depending on what a child believes it means. Kids don't hear silence as neutral. They fill it with their own interpretations.

This is why environment isn't about saying the right thing. It's about consistency.

When children know what to expect emotionally, they relax. When reactions feel unpredictable, they brace themselves.

Golf already demands enough emotional regulation. Children shouldn't have to manage the emotional climate around it, too.

One of the most damaging patterns I see in junior golf is when adults unintentionally make children responsible for adult emotions.

A parent invests time, money, and energy. A child struggles. The disappointment is real. Even when parents try to hide it, children feel it.

Suddenly, the child isn't just playing golf. They're managing expectations.

This is where anxiety enters the picture.

An anxious child doesn't lack talent. They lack safety.

They swing carefully instead of confidently.

They avoid risk instead of adapting.

They fear mistakes instead of learning from them.

Over time, this environment teaches children that golf is something to survive rather than enjoy.

Creating the right environment doesn't mean removing challenge. Golf should be challenging. Growth requires discomfort. The difference is whether that discomfort feels supported or threatening.

Supportive environments allow struggle without consequence. Threatening environments attach meaning to failure.

Children who feel supported try again. Children who

feel threatened protect themselves.

Parents often ask how to be supportive without being permissive. The answer lies in separating *expectations* from *emotions*.

You can expect effort without expecting perfection.

You can value improvement without demanding results.

You can care deeply without reacting deeply.

This balance takes practice.

I remember a parent who told me they stopped talking about golf entirely after tournaments. No analysis. No praise. No disappointment. Just space.

At first, it felt uncomfortable. The parent worried it looked like disengagement.

What actually happened was freedom.

The child began processing rounds independently. Confidence stabilized. Curiosity returned. Golf stopped bleeding into every part of life.

This wasn't neglect. It was trust.

Children thrive when golf stays in its lane.

When practice stays at practice.

When competition stays at competition.

When home stays safe.

This doesn't mean you don't care. It means you're choosing where energy belongs.

Parents who create clear emotional boundaries around golf give their children permission to grow without fear.

Time for Reflection

Pause here.

Think about the emotional environment surrounding golf in your home.

What does your child expect after a difficult round?

What tone do they anticipate in the car?

What reaction feels most familiar to them?

On the next page, describe what you believe your child experiences emotionally around golf, not what you intend, but what they likely feel.

This isn't about blame. It's about clarity.

The environment children experience shapes how they respond to challenge far beyond golf.

Kids who feel emotionally safe develop resilience. They recover faster. They take risks. They stay engaged longer.

Kids who feel pressure develop coping strategies that limit growth. They play to win instead of playing to learn.

Neither outcome is permanent, but environment nudges the trajectory.

A Commitment Worth Making

Before the next tournament or practice stretch, choose one environmental shift you will protect.

Maybe it's committing to neutral car rides.

Maybe it's waiting for your child to start golf conversations.

Maybe it's separating your emotions from their performance.

On the next page, write down one specific change you'll make to the environment around golf.

Sign and date it.

This commitment isn't about perfection. It's about intention.

Children don't need perfect environments.

They need predictable ones.

They need to know that mistakes don't threaten love, connection, or support. They need to know that golf is something they *do*, not something they *are*.

When the environment feels safe, children grow braver.

When they grow braver, learning accelerates.

And when learning accelerates, performance eventually follows.

Chapter 4

THE PARENT'S ROLE IN YOUTH GOLF

MOST PARENTS NEVER INTENDED to become part of their child's golf journey.

They signed their child up because it looked fun. Because a friend played. Because golf felt like something they could share. Somewhere along the way, without realizing when it happened, they became more involved than they ever planned to be.

They started learning terminology.

They started watching swing videos.

They started paying attention to scores, rankings, and results.

And with that involvement came responsibility, sometimes more than they were prepared for.

Parents often ask, "What exactly is my role in all of this?"

It's a reasonable question. And it's also one of the most misunderstood aspects of junior golf.

The parent's role is not to coach.

This surprises many people, especially those who are capable, knowledgeable, or deeply invested. Parents often believe that because they care the most, they should also do the most. They assume being more involved will help their child improve faster.

But in junior golf, the parent's greatest value is not instruction. It's stability.

Golf is an unstable game. Scores fluctuate. Confidence rises and falls. Progress is uneven. Children need something steady within that instability, and that steadiness does not come from technique.

It comes from relationship.

Children experience golf through the lens of connection.

They don't just feel missed shots, they feel reactions. They don't just process outcomes, they interpret meaning. Over time, they build internal stories about what their golf performance says about them and what it says about their place in the world.

Parents are central to that story.

A child doesn't need a parent who understands the golf swing. They need a parent who understands *them*.

This is where many well-meaning parents unknowingly overstep. They correct swings, offer strategy, and analyze rounds not because they want control, but because they want to help. Unfortunately, children rarely experience this as help.

They experience it as pressure.

I've watched children glance back after shots hundreds of times. Rarely are they looking for advice. They're looking for reassurance. They want to know if the relationship is intact.

When parents respond with instruction, the message received isn't guidance, it's evaluation.

Over time, children learn that performance and approval are connected. Even subtly, this connection changes how they play. They swing to avoid mistakes rather than to create shots. They manage outcomes instead of trusting instincts.

Golf becomes heavier than it needs to be.

The parent's role is not to remove challenge.

Golf should be challenging. Growth requires discomfort. The issue is not difficulty, it's emotional weight.

Parents serve best as emotional anchors. They provide calm when things go wrong. They keep perspective when frustration rises. They remind children, through actions more than words, that a bad round does not change who they are.

This role is quiet. And because it's quiet, it often feels invisible.

But it's powerful.

Many parents struggle because they feel torn between being supportive and being accountable. They worry that if they don't say something, they're letting their child down. If they don't push, they're holding them back.

What children actually need is not constant feedback, it's trust.

Trust that learning is happening even when results lag.

Trust that effort matters even when scores don't reflect

it.

Trust that development unfolds over time, not weekends.

Parents who trust the process give children permission to do the same.

I once worked with a parent who decided to stop offering any feedback after rounds. No analysis. No correction. No praise tied to performance. Just presence.

At first, it felt uncomfortable. The parent worried it looked like disengagement.

What happened instead was growth.

The child began talking more openly about rounds. They processed mistakes without defensiveness. Confidence stabilized. Golf felt lighter.

The parent hadn't stepped away. They had stepped back.

That distinction matters.

Parents also underestimate how much modeling they do.

Children watch how adults handle frustration,

disappointment, and uncertainty. They learn whether emotions are managed or projected. Whether pressure is internalized or released.

A parent's response to adversity teaches more than any lesson ever could.

When adults stay calm, children learn calm.

When adults spiral, children learn fear.

This is not about perfection. Every parent has emotional moments. What matters is pattern, not exception.

Time for Reflection

Pause here.

Think about the moments when golf doesn't go well.

How do *you* typically respond internally?

What emotions show up first, frustration, worry, disappointment, helplessness?

On the next page, write honestly about how you experience your child's struggles in golf. Not what you say, but what you feel.

Awareness is not weakness. It's leadership.

One of the most damaging things parents can do, without realizing it, is hold children responsible for adult emotions.

Children are incredibly perceptive. They sense disappointment even when words are kind. They feel urgency even when voices are calm. Over time, they adapt by managing emotions that don't belong to them.

This adaptation limits freedom.

Parents who separate their emotions from their child's performance create space for learning. They show children that golf outcomes are manageable, not threatening.

This is where real resilience begins.

The parent's role is also to protect balance.

Golf is demanding. It can consume schedules, conversations, and identity if allowed to. Children need space to be more than golfers. They need relationships, play, rest, and variety.

Parents set this tone.

When golf stays in its lane, children stay curious. When golf takes over everything, burnout creeps in, even for talented players.

Balance isn't about doing less. It's about protecting perspective.

A Commitment Worth Making

Before the next tournament stretch or practice block, consider making this commitment:

I will focus on being my child's safest place, not their loudest coach.

On the next page, write down one way you can show up more as a stabilizer than an instructor. This might be fewer words after rounds. It might be calmer body language. It might be letting your child lead conversations about golf.

Sign and date the page.

This commitment isn't about withdrawing support. It's about refining it.

Parents play a role in junior golf that no coach can replace.

They shape how the game feels.

They shape how mistakes are experienced.

They shape whether golf becomes a source of growth or anxiety.

Children don't need parents who know everything about golf. They need parents who know when to step in, and when to step back.

When parents provide stability, children learn courage.

When children learn courage, growth follows.

Quietly.

Gradually.

Lastingly.

Chapter 5

Making Practice Fun and Effective

Most parents believe practice should look serious.

Quiet focus. Repetition. Structure. Purpose.

When they see kids laughing, competing, or improvising, a quiet concern creeps in: *Are they actually getting better?*

This belief, that practice must look disciplined to be effective, is one of the most common misunderstandings in junior golf. And it's one of the reasons many children lose joy long before they lose potential.

Children don't avoid hard work. They avoid meaningless work.

When practice feels alive, improvement follows

naturally. When practice feels like obligation, learning slows, even when effort increases.

The idea of practice often changes the moment competition enters the picture.

Early on, kids practice because it's fun. They hit balls. They chase targets. They invent challenges. Improvement happens without being measured.

Then tournaments arrive.

Suddenly practice becomes preparation. Sessions become longer. Repetition replaces exploration. Adults begin tracking outcomes instead of experiences.

Practice stops being something children *want* to do and becomes something they feel they *should* do.

That shift is subtle, but powerful.

I've seen countless young players who practiced constantly yet struggled to improve. I've also seen players who practiced less, but practiced differently, and surpassed peers who spent far more time on the range.

The difference was never discipline.

It was engagement.

Children learn best when practice demands attention without demanding perfection. When tasks are challenging but playful. When failure feels informative instead of discouraging.

The brain learns faster when curiosity leads the way.

When practice becomes rigid, children start swinging to repeat instead of swinging to adapt.

They chase "good swings" instead of learning how to respond to imperfect ones. They rehearse mechanics instead of developing feel. On the range, this can look productive. On the course, it often falls apart.

Golf doesn't reward repetition. It rewards adaptability.

The course never presents the same shot twice. Lies change. Wind shifts. Pressure fluctuates. Practice that doesn't prepare children for variability leaves them unprepared when it matters most.

This is why some kids look incredible in practice and uncomfortable in competition.

Parents often assume that making practice effective means making it harder.

More balls.

More structure.

More instruction.

But harder is not always better.

Better is better.

Better practice feels intentional without feeling heavy. It challenges attention, not patience. It builds skill without draining enthusiasm.

Children who enjoy practice want to practice more, without being asked.

That matters.

One of the most effective practice sessions I ever watched looked nothing like a lesson.

A group of kids competed to hit different trajectories into a target zone. They argued about rules. They laughed. They failed repeatedly. No one mentioned mechanics.

What they were actually training was feel, creativity, and adaptability, the exact skills needed on the course.

Practice didn't feel like work.

It felt like play with purpose.

Parents sometimes worry that fun practice lacks seriousness. In reality, fun is often the gateway to deep focus.

Children concentrate longer when tasks feel meaningful. They stay engaged when challenges evolve. They push themselves when the goal feels self-driven.

This is why games work so well in junior golf, not because they're easy, but because they demand presence.

The brain learns best when it's fully engaged.

Practice also sends powerful emotional messages.

When parents hover, correct constantly, or evaluate every shot, children learn that practice is a place to be judged. When parents give space, curiosity grows.

This doesn't mean parents disengage. It means they shift roles.

Practice doesn't need commentary. It needs permission.

Permission to try.

Permission to fail.

Permission to discover.

I once worked with a player whose parents were worried because practice sessions looked unstructured. The child didn't hit many balls. They experimented. They played games. They stopped and restarted often.

The parents feared a lack of discipline.

Months later, the same child showed remarkable adaptability in competition. Bad shots didn't spiral. Missed greens didn't derail confidence. The player adjusted instinctively.

The practice had worked, just not in a way that looked familiar.

Effective practice is not about volume.

It's about intention.

Children don't need to hit hundreds of balls. They need to stay mentally present. Once attention fades, learning fades with it.

Short, engaging sessions beat long, draining ones every time.

Parents who understand this stop measuring practice by time and start paying attention to energy.

Time for Reflection

Pause here.

Think about what practice currently looks like for your child.

Does it feel like something they choose or something they endure?

Do they leave energized or depleted?

Do they talk about practice with excitement or obligation?

On the next page, write about how practice *feels* in your household. Not how it looks, but how it's experienced.

This awareness matters more than any drill ever will.

Another quiet truth about practice is this: children practice differently depending on what they believe practice is for.

If practice is about proving ability, anxiety creeps in.

If practice is about exploration, learning accelerates.

Parents shape this belief through reactions, expectations, and language.

Children learn to take risks when parents praise improvement instead of expecting perfection. When effort is valued over outcome, curiosity survives.

Practice becomes a laboratory instead of a performance.

Practice also plays a role in identity.

When children believe they must practice to maintain approval, pressure builds. When they practice to explore what they're capable of, confidence grows.

The goal is not to make practice easier. It's to make it meaningful.

Meaningful practice builds skills that last, because they belong to the child, not the instruction.

A Commitment Worth Making

Before the next practice cycle, consider making this commitment:

I will stop judging practice by how serious it looks and start noticing how engaged my child feels.

On the next page, write down one way you can support practice without controlling it. This might mean stepping back during sessions. It might mean letting your child design parts of practice. It might mean valuing effort without commentary.

Sign and date the page.

This commitment doesn't lower standards. It strengthens learning.

Practice should prepare children for the game they will actually play.

A game full of uncertainty.

A game that rewards adaptability.

A game that demands confidence under pressure.

When practice feels alive, children learn to trust themselves.

And when children trust themselves, improvement follows.

Not because they practiced more, but because they practiced better.

Chapter 6

Developing Feel over Mechanics

At some point in every junior golfer's journey, the word *feel* becomes confusing.

Parents hear coaches talk about it. Players are told to "trust it." Commentators reference it constantly. And yet, when children struggle, the instinct is almost always the same, to return to mechanics.

Where should the hands be?

What position should the club be in?

What went wrong in the swing?

Mechanics feel safe. They feel measurable. They give adults something concrete to hold onto when results are unpredictable.

Feel, on the other hand, is vague.

That vagueness makes parents uncomfortable, especially when performance matters.

But in golf, feel is not the opposite of skill.

It *is* the skill.

Children naturally begin with feel.

When they first pick up a club, they don't think about positions. They swing based on sensation. They learn what solid contact feels like. They notice how far the ball goes when the swing feels smooth versus forced.

This is learning in its purest form.

The problem is not that children lack feel.

The problem is that adults slowly teach them to distrust it.

As competition increases, instruction increases.

Swing thoughts multiply. Corrections arrive faster. Children begin hearing what they *should* be doing instead of noticing what they *are* doing.

Over time, they stop paying attention to sensation and start paying attention to positions.

This shift is subtle, but profound.

A child who once swung freely now pauses before pulling the club back. A player who once adjusted instinctively now freezes when something feels off. Confidence becomes conditional, dependent on whether the swing looks right.

Parents often interpret this as progress.

In reality, something essential is being lost.

Golf does not reward perfect mechanics.

It rewards effective motion under pressure.

That effectiveness comes from feel.

Feel allows players to adjust to uneven lies, changing wind, imperfect contact, and emotional stress. Mechanics alone cannot do that. Mechanics are static. Golf is not.

Children who rely only on mechanics often struggle when conditions change. Children who develop feel adapt naturally.

This is why some players with "imperfect" swings outperform players with technically beautiful ones.

They trust sensation over appearance.

I once worked with a young player whose swing mechanics changed weekly.

Parents were concerned. They worried about inconsistency. They asked if the swing needed to be "locked in."

What they didn't see was adaptability.

That child adjusted to lies instinctively. Distance control was intuitive. Misses stayed playable. Under pressure, the swing didn't disappear, it adjusted.

The mechanics looked messy.

The performance wasn't.

Parents often fear that focusing on feel means ignoring fundamentals.

It doesn't.

It means understanding that fundamentals should *support* feel, not replace it.

When mechanics become the focus, children try to control movement consciously. Conscious control slows reactions and increases tension. Under pressure, the brain cannot process complex instructions quickly enough.

This is why players often say, "I know what to do, I just can't do it."

Knowledge hasn't failed them. Timing has.

Developing feel requires trust.

Trust in the body.

Trust in experience.

Trust that learning happens without constant correction.

Children build feel through exploration, by trying different shots, experimenting with speed, and learning from outcomes without being told what went wrong.

Mistakes become information instead of evidence of failure.

This mindset is powerful.

Parents sometimes struggle here because feel cannot be measured easily.

You can't point to it. You can't capture it on video the way you can a position. Progress feels invisible.

Until it shows up on the course.

When a child handles a bad lie calmly.

When they adjust distance without instruction.

When they recover from mistakes without spiraling.

That's feel.

And it lasts.

Children who develop strong feel also develop independence.

They stop relying on adults to fix problems. They start solving challenges on their own. Confidence becomes internal rather than borrowed from feedback.

This independence is one of the greatest gifts junior golf can provide, on and off the course.

Parents don't lose influence when children develop feel.

They gain trust.

Time for Reflection

Pause here.

Think about the last time your child struggled during a round.

Did they look to you for answers, or reassurance?

Did they ask what went wrong, or simply react?

On the next page, write about how your child typically responds when things don't feel right in their swing. Do they experiment? Do they freeze? Do they seek instruction?

This reflection helps reveal whether feel is being nurtured or replaced.

When adults rush to explain every mistake, children stop listening to their bodies.

When adults allow space for experimentation, children learn faster.

This doesn't mean parents stay silent forever. It means choosing moments carefully. It means letting experience teach before instruction intervenes.

Timing matters.

Another quiet truth is that feel protects confidence.

Players who rely on mechanics panic when things fall apart. Players who rely on feel adapt. They know something will work eventually because something always has.

This belief keeps them present instead of frustrated.

Feel builds resilience.

A Commitment Worth Making

Before the next practice or competition stretch, consider making this commitment:

I will let my child discover solutions before I offer them.

On the next page, write about one situation where you usually step in quickly, after a bad shot, during practice, or between holes.

Now write how you might give your child space instead.

Sign and date the page.

This commitment doesn't remove guidance. It improves it.

Golf is too dynamic to be played from positions alone.

Children who develop feel learn how to respond, not just repeat. They learn to trust themselves under pressure. They learn that mistakes are part of the process, not proof of failure.

Mechanics may shape the swing.

Feel shapes the golfer.

When feel leads, mechanics support.

When mechanics lead, confidence suffers.

Develop feel first.

The rest will follow.

Chapter 7

GAMES THAT BUILD GOLF SKILLS

CHILDREN UNDERSTAND GAMES LONG before they understand instruction.

They know how to keep score. They know how to compete. They know how to adjust rules, negotiate outcomes, and try again when things don't go their way. Games make sense to them because games are how they've always learned.

Golf, ironically, often removes this instinct.

Somewhere between lessons and tournaments, practice becomes serious and games disappear. Adults assume that if something looks fun, it must be less effective. They worry that games distract from improvement, rather than realizing that games are often the fastest path to it.

For children, games are not a break from learning.

They *are* learning.

Watch a group of kids invent a game on the range and you'll see something remarkable.

They set targets without being told.

They argue about rules and outcomes.

They adapt when something isn't working.

They care deeply about the result, but they aren't afraid of it.

This combination matters.

Games create stakes without fear. They demand focus without tension. They allow failure without consequence. These are the exact conditions under which skill develops.

When adults remove games from practice, they often remove the very environment the brain needs to learn.

Parents sometimes assume that games are for beginners and that serious players must eventually "graduate" to structured repetition.

The opposite is true.

As competition increases, the need for adaptability increases. Games train adaptability better than repetition ever could. They prepare children for unpredictability, decision-making, and emotional regulation, skills that matter far more on the course than perfectly rehearsed mechanics.

Golf is a game.

Training it like it's anything else misses the point.

I once watched a young player struggle with wedge distance control for weeks.

Mechanical explanations didn't help. Repetition didn't help. The child grew frustrated and disengaged.

Then we turned practice into a game.

Targets were introduced. Scores were kept. Distances changed randomly. Suddenly the child was engaged, laughing, and adjusting instinctively.

Within days, distance control improved, not because of explanation, but because attention was finally present.

The brain learned because it was invited to.

Games work because they shift focus outward.

Instead of thinking about the body, children think about outcomes. Instead of controlling movement, they react to information. This external focus allows the brain to self-organize movement efficiently.

When children are locked into mechanics, learning slows. When attention shifts to targets, tasks, and challenges, learning accelerates.

Games create this shift naturally.

Parents sometimes worry that games lack discipline.

But discipline doesn't come from seriousness. It comes from engagement.

Children will work harder inside a game they care about than in a drill they don't understand. They'll repeat tasks voluntarily when they feel meaningful. They'll push through frustration when the challenge feels chosen rather than imposed.

Games don't reduce effort.

They redirect it.

Another reason games matter is emotional resilience.

Games normalize winning and losing. Children experience success and failure in rapid cycles. They learn to reset, adjust, and move on. This emotional rhythm mirrors competition far more closely than static practice ever could.

When children only practice "perfect" shots, mistakes feel catastrophic. When they practice inside games, mistakes feel expected.

That expectation changes everything.

Games also teach decision-making.

Golf is not just about execution. It's about choices, club selection, shot shape, risk tolerance, recovery options. Games simulate these decisions without pressure.

Children learn when to be aggressive.

They learn when to be conservative.

They learn how choices affect outcomes.

This learning sticks because it's experiential, not theoretical.

Parents often underestimate how much autonomy games provide.

When children help design games, set rules, and track outcomes, they take ownership. Ownership builds motivation. Motivation sustains effort.

This is why children who practice with games often practice more, without being asked.

The game pulls them in.

Time for Reflection

Pause here.

Think about your child's current practice routine.

How often does it include competition, creativity, or choice?

How often does your child get to choose their challenge?

On the next page, write about how games currently fit, or don't fit, into your child's practice.

This isn't about adding more structure. It's an opportunity to let your child refine their natural abilities.

Games also protect confidence.

When children succeed inside varied challenges, confidence becomes flexible. It doesn't depend on one swing or one outcome. They trust that something will work because something always does.

This confidence carries onto the course.

Children who grow up practicing with games recover faster from mistakes. They adapt mid-round. They stay engaged even when things go wrong.

They've trained for uncertainty.

Parents sometimes feel unsure how involved they should be during game-based practice.

The answer is simple.

Observe more.

Correct less.

Encourage effort without directing outcomes.

Games don't need commentary. They need space.

When parents resist the urge to interfere, games do the teaching.

A Commitment Worth Making

Before the next practice cycle, consider making this commitment:

I will value engagement and adaptability over repetition and appearance.

On the next page, write down one way you can support game-based practice without controlling it. This might mean letting your child invent rules, track scores, or choose challenges.

Sign and date the page.

This commitment doesn't lower standards. It raises learning.

Games don't replace skill development.

They *are* skill development.

They teach feel, decision-making, emotional regulation, and adaptability, the exact traits children need to succeed in golf and beyond.

When learning feels like a game, children stay curious.

When curiosity stays alive, growth follows.

Golf never stops being a game.

Training shouldn't forget that.

Chapter 8

Practice Sessions That Work

At some point, every parent realizes something uncomfortable.

Their child is practicing regularly.

Time is being invested.

Effort is clearly there.

And yet improvement feels inconsistent.

This is usually when parents start asking whether practice needs to be longer, stricter, or more intense. They assume the answer is more, more balls, more structure, more repetition.

But in junior golf, practice rarely fails because there isn't enough of it.

It fails because it isn't organized around how children actually learn.

Most practice sessions don't fail dramatically. They fail quietly.

Kids start strong. Attention fades. Swings become automatic. Bodies stay present, but minds drift. From the outside, it looks productive. But on the inside, where it matters for your child, learning has already stopped.

Children can hit balls for hours without getting better.

Designing effective practice sessions isn't about keeping a child busy—it's about keeping them engaged. Parents often confuse structure with rigidity.

They believe a good practice session should follow a fixed plan from start to finish. But children don't learn best inside rigid systems. They learn best inside *intentional* ones.

Intentional practice has a purpose, but it allows flexibility. It adapts to energy levels. It shifts when attention fades. It responds to curiosity instead of suppressing it.

Structure should serve learning, not control it.

I've watched short practice sessions outperform long ones again and again.

The difference wasn't talent or discipline. It was focus.

When practice is broken into meaningful segments, children stay mentally present. They can explore a challenge fully, then reset. This rhythm keeps the brain engaged without becoming overwhelmed.

When practice drags on without variation, the brain checks out, even if the body keeps swinging.

Learning requires attention. Without it, repetition becomes noise.

Another unsaid issue with ineffective practice is predictability.

Children often practice the same way, in the same place, hitting the same shots. The brain adapts quickly to predictable tasks. Once adaptation occurs, learning slows.

Golf, however, is unpredictable by nature.

Practice that never changes doesn't prepare children for the game they actually play. Practice that introduces variation teaches adaptability, creativity, and resilience.

This doesn't mean practice needs to be chaotic. It means it needs to be alive.

Parents sometimes worry that changing practice too often will confuse their child.

In reality, appropriate variation sharpens learning.

When children face new challenges, the brain stays alert. They solve problems instead of repeating motions. They build skills that transfer beyond the range.

This is why practice that looks slightly uncomfortable is often more effective than practice that looks smooth.

Smooth doesn't mean learned.

Messy doesn't mean broken.

Effective practice sessions also respect emotional bandwidth.

Children arrive at practice carrying more than clubs. They carry school stress, social dynamics, fatigue, and mood swings. Expecting them to perform at full capacity every session is unrealistic.

Good practice meets children where they are without lowering expectations.

Sometimes that means adjusting goals. Sometimes it means changing focus. Sometimes it means ending early.

Ending a session while engagement is still high does more for learning than pushing through exhaustion.

Parents often struggle with this idea because it feels like giving up.

It isn't.

It's protecting the desire to return.

Children who associate practice with energy and curiosity come back eager. Children who associate it with depletion avoid it, even if they don't say so out loud.

Practice should leave children wanting more, not relieved it's over.

Another factor parents underestimate is recovery.

Learning doesn't happen only during practice. It happens after.

The brain needs time to consolidate new information. When practice sessions are stacked too closely together without mental or physical recovery, learning blurs.

Rest is not laziness.

It's part of the process.

Parents who allow time for recovery often see more improvement than parents who chase volume.

Time for Reflection

Pause here.

Think about your child's typical practice sessions.

How long do they stay mentally engaged?

When does energy fade?

What happens when focus drops, do you try to continue sessions anyway?

On the next page, write about how your child typically enters and leaves practice. Energized. Neutral. Drained.

This awareness helps you recognize whether practice is feeding growth or draining it.

Effective practice also teaches children how to self-regulate.

When children learn to notice their own focus levels,

they begin to take ownership. They learn when to push and when to reset. This skill transfers directly to competition.

Players who know how to reset during practice learn how to reset during rounds.

Parents who allow children to develop this awareness give them a powerful tool.

Structure still matters.

The difference is *why* it exists.

Structure should guide attention, not dictate behavior. It should create boundaries that support exploration, not limit it.

When structure and flexibility coexist, practice becomes sustainable.

A Commitment Worth Making

Before the next practice cycle, consider making this commitment:

I will prioritize quality of focus over quantity of repetition.

On the next page, write one change you can make to support better practice sessions. This might mean shorter sessions, more breaks, or more variation.

Sign and date the page.

This commitment doesn't reduce effort. It improves learning.

Practice sessions that work are not louder, longer, or stricter.

They are intentional.

They are adaptive.

They respect attention, emotion, and recovery.

When practice aligns with how children actually learn, improvement becomes more consistent and more enjoyable.

Children don't need perfect practice plans.

They need practice that keeps them curious, engaged, and willing to return.

When practice works, everything else becomes easier.

Chapter 9

Building Confidence and Resilience

Confidence in junior golf is fragile.

It can appear quickly and disappear just as fast. One good round can make a child feel unstoppable. One difficult stretch can leave them questioning everything. Parents often assume confidence comes from success. They believe winning, scoring well, or playing consistently is what builds belief in ourselves.

In reality, confidence rarely works that way.

Confidence is not created by outcomes.

It is shaped by experience.

Children get an easy confidence boost when things go well. But real confidence is built by learning they can handle things when they don't go according to plan. Many young golfers look confident when they're winning. They smile easily. They swing freely. They recover quickly from mistakes. Parents relax. Adults assume the foundation is solid.

The test of confidence comes when things go wrong.

Missed shots. Bad bounces. Unfavorable conditions. A round that unravels early. These moments reveal whether confidence is internal or borrowed.

Borrowed confidence depends on results.

Internal confidence depends on trust.

Children with internal confidence don't panic when the game gets difficult. They adjust. They stay engaged. They believe something will work eventually, even if they don't know what yet.

This belief matters more than talent.

Parents often try to protect confidence by shielding children from failure.

They soften competition. They minimize disappointment. They rush in with reassurance before the child has processed the experience.

While the intention is kind, the outcome can be limiting.

Children build resilience by experiencing difficulty, surviving it, and moving past it.

When adults intervene too quickly, children miss the chance to learn that struggle is manageable. They learn to rely on external reassurance instead of internal stability.

Resilience is not taught through explanation.

It's earned through experience.

I've worked with players who lost confidence after one poor tournament and players who stayed composed through months of struggle.

The difference was not talent.

It was environment.

Children who were allowed to feel frustration without being rescued developed resilience. Children who were protected from discomfort often felt overwhelmed when challenges eventually arrived.

Parents don't help their children build resilience by eliminating adversity. They help them build it by providing a stable environment and helping them stay steady in its presence.

Confidence also has memory.

Children remember how they felt after past struggles. If those moments ended with calm, connection, and perspective, confidence deepens. If they ended with tension, disappointment, or emotional distance, confidence erodes.

Over time, children form expectations about how golf will feel.

Those expectations influence how children show up before the first shot is even hit.

Another quiet truth about confidence is that it grows slowly and fades quickly when attached to identity.

Children who believe they are "the good golfer" feel pressure to maintain that identity. When results dip, they feel like they're losing themselves. Confidence turns brittle.

Children who see golf as something they *do*, not something they *are*, adapt more easily. Their confidence bends without breaking.

Parents influence this distinction through language, reactions, and emphasis.

When praise centers on effort, curiosity, and perseverance, confidence becomes durable. When praise centers on outcomes, confidence becomes conditional.

Resilience also shows up in how children respond mid-round.

Some players spiral after a mistake. Others reset and move on. This ability is not about toughness, it's about familiarity.

Children who have practiced emotional recovery during practice and games are more prepared during competition. They've experienced frustration before. They know it passes.

This familiarity reduces fear.

Parents often wonder what to say when a child is clearly upset.

There is no perfect phrase.

What matters more is timing.

When emotions are high, explanation rarely helps. Connection does. Silence, presence, and calm reassurance create space for regulation.

Once emotions settle, reflection can follow.

Children don't need answers in the moment. They need safety.

Time for Reflection

Pause here.

Think about the last time your child struggled emotionally during golf.

How did you respond?

What emotions showed up for you?

Did you try to fix, distract, reassure, or step back?

On the next page, write about how you typically respond when your child is frustrated or disappointed in golf.

This awareness helps you see whether your presence builds resilience or dependency.

Confidence and resilience are closely linked.

Confidence allows children to stay engaged. Resilience allows them to recover when engagement falters. Together, they form the emotional foundation for long-term growth.

Parents support this foundation by staying consistent, especially when things go poorly.

Consistency builds trust.

Trust builds confidence.

Confidence supports resilience.

One of the most powerful things a parent can do is normalize struggle.

When children understand difficulty and challenges are normal, not alarming, they relax. They stop interpreting every setback as a problem. They focus on responding instead of judging.

This mindset transforms how children experience competition.

A Commitment Worth Making

Before the next competitive stretch, consider making this commitment:

I will let my child experience frustration without rushing to remove it.

On the next page, write one way you can stay present and calm when your child is upset. This might mean fewer words, slower reactions, or simply staying nearby.

Sign and date the page.

This commitment doesn't reduce support. It strengthens resilience.

Confidence in golf is not about believing they'll always succeed.

It's about trusting they can handle whatever happens.

Children who learn this lesson through golf carry it far beyond the course. They approach challenges with curiosity instead of fear. They stay engaged longer. They recover faster.

Resilience is not built in moments of ease.

It's built when adults show their children that it's possible to stay steady and supportive through difficulty.

When parents do that, children learn to do it themselves.

Chapter 10

Handling Pressure and Competition

PRESSURE DOESN'T ARRIVE LOUDLY in junior golf.

It doesn't announce itself. It doesn't always look dramatic. More often, it shows up quietly, tight shoulders on the first tee, rushed routines, hesitation over shots that normally feel automatic.

Parents often notice it before children can name it.

"He looks nervous today."

"She's pressing."

"He wants it too much."

Pressure is not a flaw. It's not weakness. And it's not something to eliminate.

Pressure is information.

The question is not whether children feel pressure. The question is whether they know how to move *through* it.

Most parents assume pressure comes from competition.

In reality, pressure usually comes from meaning.

A tournament matters because someone cares. A shot feels heavy because it represents something deeper: expectation, identity, approval, hope. Children rarely feel pressure from scoreboards alone. They feel it from what the outcome says about them.

This is why pressure increases as children progress.

They become more aware.

They understand stakes.

They sense what adults value.

Pressure grows with awareness, not ambition.

I've seen children perform freely in high-level events and tighten up in small local tournaments.

The difference wasn't importance.

It was expectation.

When children believe outcomes are being evaluated,

pressure spikes. When they believe effort and response matter more, pressure becomes manageable.

Parents influence this belief more than they realize.

Pressure also changes how the body moves.

Under pressure, the brain prioritizes safety. Movements become cautious. Tempo speeds up or slows down unnaturally. Players overcontrol actions that normally happen automatically.

Parents often respond by offering instruction.

"Slow down."

"Commit."

"Just trust it."

While well-meaning, these phrases rarely help in the moment. Under pressure, the brain cannot process new information efficiently.

What helps most is familiarity.

Children who have experienced pressure in manageable doses learn that it doesn't need to be feared. They learn that the sensation passes. They learn they can still function while uncomfortable.

This learning doesn't happen through explanation. It happens through exposure.

Competition plays a crucial role here.

Competition reveals how children respond emotionally. It exposes habits that practice hides. It shows whether skills hold up under uncertainty.

But competition should not be treated as a verdict.

When children feel that competition defines them, pressure becomes overwhelming. When competition is framed as information, pressure becomes useful.

Parents shape this framing.

I once worked with a child who panicked every time a scorecard was introduced.

The swing changed. Breathing shortened. Confidence vanished.

The child wasn't afraid of golf. They were afraid of evaluation.

Over time, the environment shifted. Scorecards were treated as neutral. Conversations focused on decisions and responses instead of numbers. The child gradually relaxed.

Nothing about the child's ability changed.

The meaning of competition did.

Pressure also intensifies when children feel responsible for adult emotions.

When parents invest deeply, whether it's emotionally, financially, or logistically, children sense it. They don't need it explained. They feel it in tone, body language, and silence.

Suddenly, pressure isn't about playing well.

It's about not letting someone down.

This weight is heavy for adults. It's overwhelming for children.

Parents don't remove pressure by pretending they don't care. They remove it by separating their emotional state from outcomes.

Children play more freely when they know love, connection, and support are stable regardless of results.

Another misconception is that children should learn to "handle pressure" by being tough.

Pressure is not handled by force. It's handled by

familiarity and regulation.

Children who are told to push through pressure often suppress emotion rather than process it. Suppression works temporarily. Over time, it leads to burnout or anxiety.

Children who are allowed to acknowledge pressure learn to regulate it.

They breathe.

They reset.

They refocus.

These skills grow slowly, but they last.

Parents often wonder what to say before competition.

There is no perfect script.

What matters most is consistency.

Children should hear messages that are predictable and grounding. When pre-competition conversations vary wildly based on expectations, children brace themselves emotionally.

Simple, steady messages work best.

Presence matters more than pep talks.

Time for Reflection

Pause here.

Think about how competition is talked about in your home.

What messages does your child hear before tournaments?

What tone follows difficult rounds?

How quickly does analysis replace connection?

On the next page, write about what competition *feels like* emotionally for your child, based on your observations, not assumptions.

This reflection helps reveal whether pressure is being magnified or moderated.

Pressure is unavoidable in golf.

What's optional is how heavy it becomes.

Children who learn that pressure is a sensation, not a signal of danger, stay engaged. They don't panic when nerves show up. They don't interpret discomfort as failure.

They play *with* pressure instead of against it.

Parents help children reach this point by staying calm when pressure appears. By normalizing nerves instead of fearing them. By allowing competition to teach lessons without attaching judgment.

A Commitment Worth Making

Before the next tournament, consider making this commitment:

I will treat competition as information, not evaluation.

On the next page, write one way you can reinforce this mindset. This might mean delaying analysis, focusing on decisions instead of scores, or simply listening more than speaking.

Sign and date the page.

This commitment doesn't remove accountability. It changes the meaning of pressure. Competition is where skills are tested, but it's also where growth is revealed.

Children don't need pressure-free environments. They need environments that teach them how to respond when pressure arrives.

When parents stay steady, children learn steadiness.

When parents separate emotion from outcome, children do the same.

Over time, pressure becomes familiar.

And familiar pressure is no longer frightening.

It's simply part of the game.

Chapter 11

WHEN CHALLENGES ARISE

NO JUNIOR GOLF JOURNEY unfolds without interruption.

At some point, often more than once, something goes wrong. Progress stalls. Confidence dips. Scores rise unexpectedly. Motivation fades. An injury appears. A child who once loved the game begins to hesitate before picking up a club.

These moments catch parents off guard, not because they are rare, but because they feel personal.

Parents often ask, "What happened?"

The harder question is, "What does this moment need?"

Challenges in junior golf don't arrive as signs of failure. They arrive as part of development. The problem is not that challenges appear, it's how quickly adults try to escape them.

Most challenges resolve over time.

They show up as frustration during practice.

As reluctance to compete.

As irritability after rounds that used to feel manageable.

Parents sense something is off before children can articulate it. This uncertainty makes adults uncomfortable. They want clarity, direction, and solutions.

The instinct is to intervene.

More lessons.

More practice.

More structure.

But many challenges don't need fixing. They need space.

One of the most common challenges parents encounter is the plateau.

Improvement slows. Scores stop dropping. The child looks the same week after week. Parents worry that development has stalled or that something has been missed.

Plateaus are not problems. They are pauses.

They occur when the brain is consolidating learning, when bodies are adjusting to growth, or when confidence is recalibrating. During these phases, progress may be invisible, but it is still happening.

Parents who panic during plateaus often disrupt them. Parents who stay patient allow the next leap to arrive naturally.

Another challenge that unsettles parents is regression.

A child who once performed well suddenly struggles. Shots that were reliable disappear. Confidence wavers. Adults fear that something has been lost.

Regression feels alarming because it contradicts expectations.

But regression is often temporary.

As children grow, physically and emotionally, old patterns stop working before new ones stabilize. This phase feels uncomfortable, but it's often necessary for advancement.

When adults rush to restore what used to work, they can delay the transition to what will work next.

Injuries present a different kind of challenge.

They interrupt momentum. They create uncertainty. They force rest when children want progress. Parents worry about lost time and lost opportunities.

Children often worry about something deeper.

They worry about falling behind.

This fear can be heavier than the injury itself.

Parents play a critical role here by reframing recovery as part of development, not a detour from it. Healing teaches patience, body awareness, and perspective, skills that matter long after the injury has healed.

When adults treat injury as a catastrophe, children internalize fear. When adults treat it as a chapter, children adapt.

Motivation dips can be equally unsettling.

A child who once begged to practice now resists. Enthusiasm fades. Parents fear burnout or loss of passion.

Sometimes motivation dips because golf has become heavy. Sometimes because life has expanded. Sometimes because the child is changing.

Not every dip in motivation means something is wrong.

Children are allowed to step back. They are allowed to question. They are allowed to need space.

Parents who force engagement often deepen resistance. Parents who allow breathing room often see curiosity return.

One of the most misunderstood challenges is emotional volatility.

Children experience emotions intensely. A missed shot can feel catastrophic. A bad round can feel personal. Parents may struggle to know when to step in and when to step back.

The goal is not to calm emotions immediately. The goal is to allow emotions to move through without escalating them.

Children who learn that emotions are safe learn to regulate them. Children who feel pressure to suppress emotions often carry them longer.

Parents sometimes feel helpless during these moments.

They want to help but don't know how. They worry that

doing nothing looks like neglect.

Doing nothing is not the same as doing nothing *wrong*.

Presence without interference is often the most powerful response.

Children need to know they are not alone, but also that they are capable.

Time for Reflection

Pause here.

Think about the most recent challenge your child faced in golf.

Was it a plateau, regression, injury, loss of motivation, or emotional struggle?

How did you respond internally?

What emotions surfaced for you?

On the next page, write about what that challenge felt like *for you*, not just for your child.

Understanding your own response helps you show up more intentionally the next time.

Challenges often reveal patterns.

Some parents move quickly to fix.

Some minimize.

Some become anxious.

Some withdraw.

None of these responses are permanent. Awareness allows choice.

Children benefit most from adults who can stay regulated when uncertainty arises.

One of the most powerful things parents can say during difficult stretches is nothing at all.

Not silence filled with tension, but silence filled with presence.

Children don't need immediate answers. They need time to process. They need to feel that struggle does not threaten connection.

When parents resist urgency, children learn patience.

A Commitment Worth Making

Before the next challenge arises, and it will, consider making this commitment:

I will respond to challenges with curiosity instead of urgency.

On the next page, write one way you can slow down your response when something feels wrong. This might mean waiting before taking action, listening longer, or asking fewer questions.

Sign and date the page.

This commitment doesn't ignore problems. It creates space to understand them.

Challenges are not interruptions in development.

They *are* development.

They teach adaptability, resilience, patience, and perspective. They reveal how children respond when things don't go as planned.

Parents who stay steady during these moments give children permission to grow through difficulty instead of around it.

Golf doesn't promise smooth journeys.

It promises lessons.

When challenges arise, the lesson is rarely about golf.

It's about learning how to stay engaged when things feel uncertain.

And that lesson lasts far beyond the course.

Chapter 12

Maintaining Long-Term Motivation

Motivation rarely disappears all at once.

It fades quietly.

A skipped practice here.

A distracted session there.

Less curiosity. Less urgency. Less excitement about things that once mattered.

Parents often notice it before children do. They sense a shift in energy, a change in tone, a subtle resistance where eagerness used to live. And when they notice it, fear follows.

"What if they're losing their passion?"

"What if we pushed too hard?"

"What if they quit?"

These questions are heavy because they feel final.

But motivation is not fragile in the way many parents believe.

It is responsive.

Children are not motivated by the same things adults are.

Adults are motivated by outcomes, timelines, and long-term goals. Children are motivated by meaning, autonomy, and connection. When those elements are present, motivation sustains itself. When they disappear, motivation erodes, even if opportunity and structure remain.

This is why children can lose motivation even while performing well.

Results alone are not enough.

One of the most common mistakes parents make is assuming motivation must be preserved at all costs.

They fill schedules.

They increase incentives.

They add pressure disguised as encouragement.

What children often need instead is space.

Motivation doesn't thrive when it's monitored constantly. It thrives when children feel ownership over their experience. When golf feels chosen instead of required, curiosity stays alive.

I've seen highly talented children walk away from the game not because they lacked ability, but because they lost agency.

Golf became something that happened *to* them instead of something they participated in. Decisions were made for them. Goals were set without them. Success was measured externally.

Over time, enthusiasm faded.

Not because they stopped loving golf, but because golf stopped feeling like theirs.

Long-term motivation depends on autonomy.

Children need to feel they have a voice in their journey. They need input on practice, competition, and goals. This doesn't mean children run the program. It means they are included in the conversation.

When children feel heard, motivation strengthens.

When they feel managed, motivation weakens.

Parents play a key role here by inviting collaboration instead of control.

Another threat to motivation is identity overload.

When children begin to believe that golf defines them, the stakes become overwhelming. Every round feels like a referendum on who they are. Every setback feels personal.

Motivation struggles under that weight.

Children stay motivated longer when golf is something they *do*, not something they *are*. They thrive when they are allowed to be students, friends, siblings, and kids, not just golfers.

Parents reinforce this balance through language and emphasis.

Motivation also ebbs during natural developmental phases.

Growth spurts. Academic pressure. Social changes. Emotional maturity. All of these influence how children engage with golf.

A dip in motivation doesn't always signal burnout. Sometimes it signals growth elsewhere.

Parents who interpret every dip as danger often overcorrect. Parents who observe calmly often see motivation return organically.

There is also a difference between discipline and desire.

Discipline can keep a child showing up. Desire determines how they engage once they're there. Long-term success requires both, but desire must lead.

Children who are forced to rely on discipline alone eventually resent the activity. Children whose desire is nurtured develop discipline naturally.

Desire cannot be forced.

It can only be protected.

Parents sometimes ask how to motivate their child during difficult stretches.

The answer is rarely to push harder.

It's to listen.

Listening restores agency. Listening communicates respect. Listening allows children to reconnect with why they started in the first place.

When children feel understood, motivation has room to breathe.

Time for Reflection

Pause here.

Think about your child's current relationship with golf.

Does it feel driven by curiosity or obligation?

Do they initiate conversations about golf, or avoid them?

Do they feel free to say they need a break?

On the next page, write honestly about what you believe is currently fueling your child's motivation, or draining it.

This reflection helps you distinguish between temporary fatigue and deeper disengagement.

Long-term motivation also depends on rest.

Rest is not the opposite of commitment. It's part of it.

Children who are never allowed to step back can't

choose to step forward. Breaks renew desire. They allow perspective to reset. They remind children that golf is one part of life, not all of it.

Parents who respect rest often see motivation return stronger.

Another important factor is celebration.

Not celebration of outcomes, but celebration of growth.

When parents notice effort, courage, resilience, and curiosity, children feel seen beyond results. Motivation becomes internal instead of performative.

Children who feel valued for who they are stay engaged longer.

A Commitment Worth Making

Before the next season or practice cycle, consider making this commitment:

I will protect my child's sense of choice within their golf journey.

On the next page, write one way you can increase your child's autonomy. This might mean involving them in scheduling, goal setting or deciding when to rest.

Sign and date the page.

This commitment doesn't reduce structure. It strengthens motivation.

Motivation is not something parents create.

It's something they protect.

Children who stay motivated over the long term are not the ones who were pushed the hardest. They're the ones who felt ownership, balance, and connection throughout the journey.

When children feel that golf belongs to them, they return to it willingly.

Again and again.

And that willingness is what sustains a lifetime in the game.

Chapter 13

Balancing Golf with Childhood

One of the quietest tensions in junior golf lives outside the ropes.

It shows up in schedules packed too tightly. In weekends that blur together. In conversations where school, friends, rest, and play slowly make room for practice sessions and tournaments.

Parents don't usually notice this shift as it happens. It feels gradual. Reasonable. Each decision makes sense on its own.

Taken together, though, the balance begins to tip.

And when balance tips for too long, something important gets lost.

Childhood is not a phase to rush through.

It is not an inconvenience on the way to success. It is the foundation on which long-term performance is built.

Children need more than skill development to thrive. They need freedom, play, rest, imagination, and relationships that exist outside of golf. These elements don't compete with development.

They support it.

Parents often feel torn.

They want to give their child every opportunity. They worry that stepping back might mean falling behind. They fear that balance could be mistaken for lack of commitment.

In junior golf culture, busy schedules are often celebrated. More practice is equated with more dedication. More competition is seen as ambition.

But children don't experience busyness as ambition.

They experience it as pressure.

I've worked with children who practiced constantly yet struggled to stay engaged. I've also worked with children who practiced less, played more, and stayed curious longer.

The difference wasn't desire.

It was space.

Children who have space to be kids return to golf with energy. Children who feel consumed by golf begin to withdraw, even if results remain strong.

Balance doesn't weaken development.

It protects it.

Golf demands focus, patience, and emotional regulation. These qualities don't develop in isolation. They are shaped through a full life.

School challenges teach problem-solving. Friendships teach communication. Free play teaches creativity. Downtime teaches self-regulation.

When golf crowds out these experiences, development becomes narrow. Performance may rise briefly, but resilience suffers.

Children who grow up balanced adapt better to pressure. They recover faster from setbacks. They stay connected to the game longer.

Parents sometimes worry that allowing balance sends the wrong message.

That it suggests golf isn't important.

Children don't interpret balance that way.

They interpret it as trust.

Trust that golf will be there.

Trust that their worth isn't tied to performance.

Trust that they are allowed to grow fully, not just athletically.

That trust strengthens commitment, not weakens it.

Another subtle cost of imbalance is identity.

When golf dominates life, children begin to define themselves by results. Success feels validating. Struggle feels threatening. Emotional swings intensify.

Balanced children experience golf as one meaningful part of a larger life. When rounds go poorly, disappointment exists, but it doesn't consume them.

This perspective protects mental health and long-term motivation.

Parents also underestimate the role of unstructured time.

Unstructured time is where children process experiences. It's where curiosity resurfaces. It's where intrinsic motivation grows.

When every moment is scheduled, children stop listening to themselves. They rely on external direction instead of internal signals.

Balance restores that connection.

I once worked with a family who deliberately reduced their child's golf schedule for a season.

Fewer tournaments. Shorter practices. More time for school events, friends, and rest.

Results dipped initially. Parents worried.

Then something shifted.

The child returned to practice energized. Focus improved. Enjoyment returned. Performance stabilized, not because of more golf, but because of better balance.

Nothing had been lost.

Something had been protected.

Time for Reflection

Pause here.

Think about your child's weekly rhythm.

How much of their time is structured?

How much is unstructured?

Where does golf fit among school, friends, family, and rest?

On the next page, write honestly about whether your child's life feels balanced, or crowded.

This reflection isn't about guilt. It's about awareness.

Balance also means listening when children communicate fatigue, even when they don't use words. Irritability. Withdrawal. Resistance. Loss of enthusiasm. These are often signals, not problems.

Parents who listen early can adjust gently. Parents who wait until burnout appears often need to make bigger changes. Small adjustments made early preserve joy.

Another important part of balance is seasonality.

Golf doesn't have to be intense all the time. There can

be seasons of focus and seasons of rest. Seasons of competition and seasons of play.

Children benefit from these rhythms. They prevent overload and renew interest.

Balance is not static. It shifts as children grow.

A Commitment Worth Making

Before the next season or scheduling decision, consider making this commitment:

I will protect my child's time to be a child, not just a golfer.

On the next page, write one small change you can make to restore balance. This might mean fewer tournaments, more free weekends, or simply more unstructured time.

Sign and date the page.

This commitment doesn't reduce opportunity. It protects sustainability.

Golf can be a powerful part of childhood. It can teach patience, resilience, focus, and integrity. But it should not replace childhood itself.

Children who grow up balanced become adults who stay connected—to the game and to themselves.

When golf fits into life instead of consuming it, children stay curious longer.

And curiosity is what keeps them playing.

Chapter 14

THE COMPETITION QUESTION

FEW TOPICS CREATE AS much quiet tension in junior golf as competition.

When to start.

How often to play.

What level is appropriate.

Whether a child is "ready."

Parents rarely ask these questions out loud at first. They think about them on long drives home. They compare schedules. They watch other children advance, or struggle, and wonder what it means for their own.

Competition feels like a gateway. Step through it at the right time and growth accelerates. Step through it too early or too often and something important can fracture.

The challenge is there is no universal answer.

Competition is not inherently good or bad.

It is simply a tool.

Like any tool, its value depends on how and when it's used.

Competition can sharpen focus, build resilience, and reveal growth. It can also amplify pressure, expose insecurity, and overwhelm developing confidence.

The difference is not talent.

It's readiness.

Parents often assume readiness is about skill.

Can my child score well enough?

Do they hit it far enough?

Can they keep up?

Those questions matter, but they are not the most important ones.

Readiness is emotional before it is technical.

A child who can handle frustration, recover from mistakes, and stay engaged during difficulty is far more prepared for competition than a child with superior mechanics but fragile confidence.

Competition tests emotions long before it tests skill.

I've seen children dominate local events and unravel under slightly higher stakes. I've also seen children struggle early, learn from experience, and grow into competitors who trust themselves deeply.

The difference was not ability.

It was how competition was introduced and framed.

When competition is treated as a verdict, pressure skyrockets. When it's treated as information, learning accelerates.

Parents influence this framing more than any scoreboard ever could.

One of the most common mistakes in junior golf is over-competition.

More events. More travel. More exposure. More pressure.

Parents fear that slowing down means falling behind. They worry that saying no now means missing opportunities later.

What often happens instead is emotional fatigue.

Children stop processing experiences. Rounds blur together. Learning flattens. Joy fades quietly.

Competition without recovery doesn't build resilience.

It drains it.

Another quiet risk of over-competition is identity attachment.

When children compete constantly, results begin to define them. Success feels validating. Struggle feels threatening. Emotional swings intensify.

Children who compete less frequently often process experiences more deeply. They reflect. They integrate lessons. They return stronger.

Space matters.

Parents sometimes assume competition is the best teacher.

It can be, but only when children are ready to learn from it.

If a child leaves competition feeling confused, ashamed, or defeated without understanding why, the lesson isn't growth.

It's fear.

Fear lingers.

Parents who pay attention to emotional responses after competition gain valuable insight into readiness. Not readiness to win, but readiness to learn.

Another important aspect of competition is choice.

Children who feel forced into competition experience pressure differently than children who feel invited into it. Ownership changes everything.

When children help decide when and where to compete, engagement increases. Pressure becomes manageable. Motivation stabilizes.

This doesn't mean children control the schedule completely. It means they are part of the conversation.

Collaboration builds commitment.

Parents also underestimate how much competition culture influences children.

Scoreboards. Rankings. Comparisons. Conversations overheard between adults. All of it shapes how children interpret success and failure.

Parents who stay grounded amid competitive noise give children an anchor. They remind them, through words and behavior, that golf is a journey, not a race.

That message matters more than placement.

Time for Reflection

Pause here.

Think about your child's current competition schedule.

How often are they competing?

How do they feel afterward, energized, drained, reflective, anxious?

What emotions show up most consistently?

On the next page, write about how competition currently impacts your child emotionally, not just technically.

This reflection helps reveal whether competition is serving development or overshadowing it.

Competition should stretch children, not strain them.

A healthy competitive experience leaves children tired but curious. Frustrated but engaged. Motivated to return, not relieved to stop.

When competition consistently leaves children emotionally depleted, something needs adjustment.

Adjustment is not failure.

It's wisdom.

Another overlooked aspect of competition is timing within a season.

Back-to-back events with no space to process can dull learning. Strategic pauses allow integration. Reflection deepens understanding.

Parents who schedule with intention often see more growth than parents who chase volume.

Less can be more, when chosen thoughtfully.

A Commitment Worth Making

Before the next competition decision, consider making this commitment:

I will choose competition based on readiness and

learning, not comparison or fear.

On the next page, write one way you can adjust your approach to competition. This might mean fewer events, more recovery time, or clearer framing around outcomes.

Sign and date the page.

This commitment doesn't limit opportunity. It protects development.

Competition is not the destination in junior golf.

It's one of many classrooms.

When used wisely, it teaches resilience, focus, and self-awareness. When rushed or overused, it teaches fear.

Parents who view competition as a tool, not a measure, give children the best chance to grow.

Children don't need more tournaments to become great golfers.

They need the *right* competitive experiences at the *right* time.

And when those experiences are chosen with care,

competition becomes what it was always meant to be.

A place to learn.

Chapter 15

Technology and Modern Golf

Junior golf today looks nothing like it did a generation ago.

Launch monitors line driving ranges. Swing videos play back instantly on phones. Stats track everything from fairways hit to putting averages. Apps promise insights, fixes, and faster improvement.

Parents often feel caught in the middle.

On one hand, technology feels helpful. Objective. Modern. It offers clarity in a game that can feel confusing. On the other hand, too much information can overwhelm children who are still learning how to trust themselves.

The question is no longer whether technology belongs

in junior golf.

It's how, and when, it should be used.

Technology is not inherently good or bad.

It is a tool.

Like competition, its value depends entirely on context. Used thoughtfully, technology can support learning, awareness, and feedback. If overused, it can create dependency, anxiety, and distraction.

The difference is not sophistication.

It's intention.

Many parents turn to technology during moments of uncertainty.

A child struggles. Progress stalls. Confidence dips. Numbers feel reassuring because they appear objective. They offer explanations when emotions run high.

But numbers don't tell the whole story.

A launch monitor can measure speed, spin, and direction. It cannot measure confidence, curiosity, or emotional readiness. A swing video can show positions. It cannot show trust.

Parents who rely too heavily on technology risk missing the most important signals.

Children experience technology differently than adults.

Adults often see data as neutral information. Children experience it as evaluation. Numbers can quickly become judgments. Rankings can feel like identity. Comparisons can feel personal.

When children begin measuring themselves constantly, they stop listening to their bodies. Feel is replaced by feedback. Instinct gives way to analysis.

This doesn't mean technology should be avoided.

It means it should be introduced carefully.

I've seen young players become obsessed with numbers they don't fully understand.

They chase swing speed at the expense of control. They fixate on launch angles without knowing how to adjust naturally. They compare stats to others without context.

Confidence suffers.

Not because technology failed, but because it arrived too soon.

Technology works best when it confirms learning rather than drives it.

When children explore, experiment, and feel changes first, technology can help reinforce understanding. When technology leads the process, children often disengage from sensation and rely on external validation.

The order matters.

Feel first.

Feedback second.

Parents who understand this sequence protect development.

Another quiet cost of overusing technology is distraction.

Golf already demands attention. Adding screens, constant feedback, and performance metrics can fragment focus. Children may become more concerned with what the device says than what the shot requires.

The game becomes mediated.

Children stop playing golf and start monitoring golf.

This shift reduces creativity and adaptability, two traits essential for long-term success.

Parents also face pressure from comparison.

When other families use advanced tools, it's natural to wonder if you're falling behind. Technology creates visibility. Stats circulate. Progress appears measurable.

But visibility is not the same as growth.

Children develop at different rates. What looks impressive on paper may not translate under pressure. What looks unremarkable may be building deep foundations.

Technology doesn't change this reality.

Another challenge is access.

Not every family has the same resources. Not every child benefits equally from the same tools. When technology becomes a status symbol rather than a learning aid, children absorb unintended messages about worth and opportunity.

Parents can counter this by emphasizing effort, curiosity, and experience over equipment.

Golf has always rewarded skill over gear.

Technology can also influence relationships.

When parents become interpreters of data, the dynamic shifts. Conversations move from connection to analysis. Children may feel constantly assessed, even when improvement is happening.

Parents who maintain emotional distance from technology preserve trust.

Technology should support the journey, not define it.

Time for Reflection

Pause here.

Think about how technology currently fits into your child's golf experience.

How often is feedback delivered through devices?

Consider how your child responds to data, are they curious, anxious, or indifferent?

Does technology spark conversation or shut it down?

On the next page, write about whether technology is currently enhancing your child's learning, or distracting from it.

There is no right answer. Only awareness.

Technology is most powerful when children choose to use it.

When children ask questions, seek feedback, and explore data voluntarily, engagement increases. When technology is imposed, resistance grows.

Choice changes everything.

Parents who allow children to lead technology use see better outcomes, both emotionally and technically.

Consider timing and development of skills before introducing technology.

Early stages benefit more from play, exploration, and feel. Later stages can benefit from precision and feedback. Introducing advanced tools too early can limit instinct. Introducing them thoughtfully later can refine skill.

There is no rush.

The game will be there.

A Commitment Worth Making

Before introducing a new device, app, or metric, consider making this commitment:

I will use technology to support learning, not replace it.

On the next page, write one way you can shift how technology is used. This might mean reducing frequency, changing timing, or letting your child initiate feedback.

Sign and date the page.

This commitment doesn't reject progress. It protects balance.

Technology will continue to evolve.

Devices will become faster, smarter, and more accessible. Data will become more detailed. Tools will promise quicker results.

What will not change is how children learn.

They still need curiosity.

They still need safety.

They still need trust in their own feel.

Parents who keep these priorities at the center can use technology wisely, without letting it take over.

When technology serves the child, learning deepens.

When technology leads the child, confidence suffers.

The difference is not the tool.

It's the hand that holds it.

Chapter 16

Building Your Support Team

No junior golfer succeeds alone.

Even the most independent, driven players are shaped by the people around them. Coaches, parents, peers, teachers, and mentors all contribute to how the game is experienced and understood. When these roles are clear and aligned, development feels supported. When they blur or conflict, progress becomes confusing.

Parents often feel responsible for assembling this team without a guide.

Who should coach my child?

How involved should I be?

When should other voices be invited in, or kept out?

These questions matter, not because there is one perfect answer, but because clarity protects children.

A support team works best when every role is defined.

The most common mistake in junior golf is not a lack of support, it's overlap.

Parents try to coach.

Coaches try to parent.

Peers become benchmarks.

Advice arrives from too many directions at once.

Children become the managers of adult expectations.

This is exhausting.

The coach's role is to guide development.

A good coach sees patterns over time. They understand how skills evolve. They know when to push and when to pause. Their value lies not just in knowledge, but in perspective.

Parents sometimes evaluate coaches based on immediate results. But development doesn't operate on short timelines. The best coaches often create lasting changes that may not show up right away.

Trust matters.

When parents undermine a coach's role, by correcting swings, questioning decisions in front of the child, or introducing conflicting instruction, children feel caught in the middle.

Confusion replaces confidence.

The parent's role is different.

Parents provide emotional stability. They protect perspective. They remind children who they are beyond golf. This role is powerful precisely because it is not technical.

When parents try to become coaches, they risk losing their greatest influence.

Children need at least one relationship in golf that is safe from evaluation. Parents are best positioned to provide that.

Peers also play a role, often a larger one than adults realize.

Children compare themselves constantly. They absorb attitudes, habits, and beliefs from teammates and competitors. Peers can motivate or discourage, depending on the environment.

Parents can't control peer influence, but they can help children interpret it. When comparisons arise, parents who redirect focus inward help children stay grounded.

Peers are part of the journey, not the scoreboard.

Another often-overlooked member of the support team is the child themselves.

Children need to feel included in decisions about their development. When adults make choices without them, motivation weakens. When children feel heard, engagement strengthens.

This doesn't mean children run the program. It means they understand the *why* behind decisions.

Understanding builds trust.

Support teams also evolve.

The people a child needs at eight are different from the people they need at fourteen. Coaches change. Priorities shift. Responsibilities grow.

Parents who allow the support team to adapt over time avoid unnecessary conflict. Parents who cling to early structures often create tension.

Flexibility is strength.

I've seen children thrive when their support team communicated clearly.

Parents trusted coaches. Coaches respected family values. Expectations were consistent. Children knew where to turn for guidance and where they were free to explore.

I've also seen children struggle when messages conflicted.

One voice emphasized patience. Another emphasized urgency. One valued learning. Another demanded results.

The child tried to satisfy everyone.

No one benefited.

Parents often worry that stepping back from certain roles means disengagement.

It doesn't.

It means specialization.

When each person stays in their lane, support becomes stronger, not weaker.

Children feel held instead of pulled.

Time for Reflection

Pause here.

Think about the people currently influencing your child's golf journey.

Who provides technical guidance?

Who provides emotional support?

Who influences expectations, directly or indirectly?

On the next page, write about whether these roles feel clear or overlapping.

Clarity reduces stress, for children and adults alike.

Support teams also communicate values.

Children notice how adults speak about coaches, tournaments, competitors, and setbacks. These conversations shape how children interpret success and failure.

Parents who model respect, even during a disagreement, teach emotional maturity. Parents who criticize openly teach defensiveness.

Children learn how to navigate relationships by watching adults navigate theirs.

Another important role on the support team is someone outside golf.

Teachers, family members, mentors, or friends who see the child beyond performance provide balance. They remind children that identity is broader than results.

These voices matter more than parents often realize.

A Commitment Worth Making

Before the next season or coaching decision, consider making this commitment:

I will protect clear roles within my child's support team.

On the next page, write one way you can strengthen role clarity. This might mean stepping back from instruction, improving communication with coaches, or limiting conflicting input.

Sign and date the page.

This commitment doesn't reduce involvement. It refines it.

A strong support team doesn't overwhelm children with advice.

It surrounds them with clarity.

When children know who to listen to, and when, they relax. They trust the process. They stay engaged.

Parents don't need to build the perfect team.

They need to build a *clear* one.

When roles are respected, development accelerates.

And when development is supported, children find their way, on the course and beyond.

Chapter 17

Life Lessons Through Golf

Long after scorecards are lost and swings have changed, golf leaves something behind.

It leaves habits.

It leaves perspectives.

It leaves lessons that quietly shape how children see the world and themselves.

Parents' initial impressions about junior golf are trophies, scholarships, or competitive success. Over time, many realize something deeper is happening. Golf becomes a classroom for life, not because it teaches perfection, but because it teaches response.

How children respond to difficulty.

How they handle uncertainty.

How they recover when things don't go their way.

These lessons matter far beyond the course.

Golf teaches patience in a way few activities can.

Improvement is slow. Feedback is delayed. Effort doesn't always produce immediate reward. Children learn quickly that progress requires time, and that frustration is part of the process.

Parents who allow children to sit inside this discomfort without rescuing them help build patience that transfers everywhere. School challenges. Relationships. Long-term goals.

Children learn that persistence isn't loud.

It's steady.

Golf also teaches accountability.

There are no teammates to hide behind. No excuses that last. Each shot belongs to the player who hit it. This responsibility can feel heavy, but it's also empowering.

Children who learn to take ownership of mistakes without shame develop confidence. They stop fearing errors and start learning from them.

Parents shape these lessons by how they react.

When mistakes are treated as learning opportunities, accountability feels safe. When mistakes are met with disappointment, accountability turns into fear.

Another powerful lesson golf teaches is emotional regulation.

The game provokes emotion constantly. Frustration. Excitement. Anxiety. Relief. Children experience emotional swings in compressed time frames.

Golf doesn't require children to suppress emotion. It requires them to manage it.

Children who learn to breathe, reset, and refocus carry those skills into exams, relationships, and stressful situations. They learn that emotion doesn't need to dictate behavior.

Parents reinforce this lesson through modeling.

Calm adults teach calm children.

Golf also introduces humility.

No matter how talented a child is, the game eventually

humbles them. Bad rounds arrive. Progress stalls. Limitations appear.

Children who learn humility without losing confidence develop resilience. They understand that setbacks don't define them, they refine them.

Parents play a key role here by separating worth from performance.

Humility without shame builds character.

Another life lesson golf teaches is decision-making.

Every shot is a choice. Risk versus safety. Aggression versus restraint. Commitment versus doubt. Children learn decisions have consequences, and not every outcome can be controlled.

This understanding builds maturity.

Children stop blaming circumstances and start focusing on response. They learn to evaluate choices without judgment and adjust next time.

Golf trains reflection naturally.

Golf also teaches independence.

Over time, children stop relying on adults to solve

problems. They learn to assess situations, trust instincts, and adapt on their own.

This independence is fragile early and powerful later.

Parents who resist the urge to intervene give children space to develop self-reliance. Parents who step in too quickly unintentionally slow this process.

Independence grows when trust is given.

Parents often worry about what happens if their child doesn't "make it" in golf.

What they often don't realize is that golf has already succeeded if these lessons take root.

Not every child will play competitively forever. Not every child will earn recognition or opportunity through the game.

But every child can carry the lessons forward.

Time for Reflection

Pause here.

Think about what you hope your child gains from golf beyond rankings or results.

What qualities do you hope they develop?

What challenges do you hope they learn to handle?

What type of person do you hope they become?

On the next page, write about the life lessons you believe golf is currently teaching your child.

This reflection helps clarify what truly matters.

Life lessons are absorbed through experience, not instruction.

Children don't learn resilience because someone explains it. They learn it because they live it. They don't learn patience because they're told to be patient. They learn it because progress demands it.

Parents don't need to teach these lessons directly.

They need to provide an environment where learning can happen.

Golf also teaches perspective.

Children learn that effort doesn't guarantee outcome. That success can be temporary. That failure can be informative. These realizations build emotional intelligence.

Children who understand this don't crumble under pressure. They adapt.

Perspective creates stability.

A Commitment Worth Making

Before the next season or transition, consider making this commitment:

I will value the life lessons golf teaches as much as the results it produces.

On the next page, write one way you can reinforce this perspective. This might mean celebrating resilience, acknowledging growth, or reframing setbacks.

Sign and date the page.

This commitment doesn't diminish ambition. It deepens meaning.

Golf is not just a sport.

It is a mirror.

It reflects how children handle challenge, how adults respond to uncertainty, and how growth unfolds over time. The lessons it offers are subtle but enduring.

When parents focus on the person being shaped, not just the golfer being developed, the journey becomes richer.

And regardless of where golf leads, those lessons remain.

Long after the final round is played.

Chapter 18

Raising a Lifelong Champion

When parents are first introduced to junior golf, they often think they know what success looks like.

It looks like trophies on shelves.

It looks like lower scores.

It looks like progress that can be measured, tracked, and compared.

Those markers aren't wrong, but they're incomplete.

Over time, many parents begin to realize the most meaningful victories don't always show up on scoreboards. They show up in quieter moments. In how children respond to adversity. In how they talk to themselves after mistakes. In whether they want to return to the game willingly, or feel relieved when it ends.

This is where the idea of raising a lifelong champion begins to change.

A lifelong champion is not defined by how early they succeed.

They are defined by how long they stay connected.

Connected to curiosity.

Connected to effort.

Connected to growth.

Some lifelong champions compete at high levels. Some play recreationally. Some step away from competition altogether and return later in life. What unites them is not outcome, it's relationship.

They have a healthy relationship with the game and with themselves.

Parents often worry that easing pressure means lowering standards.

In reality, the opposite is true.

Children who feel safe to struggle develop higher standards internally. They become self-motivated. They care deeply, not because they're afraid to disappoint, but because they want to grow.

External pressure produces compliance.

Internal motivation produces commitment.

Lifelong champions are internally driven.

Throughout this book, one theme has appeared again and again.

Children don't need perfect instruction.

They don't need constant correction.

They don't need adults who have all the answers.

They need adults who understand development.

They need environments that feel safe.

They need relationships that aren't conditional.

They need space to explore, fail, adapt, and grow.

Parents are the stewards of that environment.

Raising a lifelong champion doesn't require you to do more.

It often requires you to do less, but with more intention.

Less talking after rounds.

Less comparison.

Less urgency when things go wrong.

More listening.

More patience.

More trust in the process.

This balance is not passive. It's purposeful.

There will be moments when you doubt yourself.

Moments when other families seem to be moving faster.

Moments when results lag behind effort.

Moments when your child struggles and you want to intervene.

These moments don't mean you're failing.

They mean you're parenting inside uncertainty.

And uncertainty is where growth lives.

One of the greatest gifts you can give your child through golf is perspective.

Perspective that effort matters more than outcome.

Perspective that growth is not linear.

Perspective that who they are matters more than how they score.

When children absorb this perspective, they become resilient, not just in golf, but in life.

They learn to trust themselves.

They learn to stay engaged through challenge.

They learn to carry confidence without arrogance and humility without shame.

That is championship character.

Parents sometimes ask how they'll know if they did it right.

The answer is not found in rankings or results.

You'll know when your child can experience disappointment without losing themselves.

You'll know when they take ownership of their journey.

You'll know when they play because they want to, not because they feel obligated.

You'll know when golf becomes a teacher instead of a test.

A Final Moment for Reflection

Pause here.

Think back to why you introduced your child to golf in the first place.

What did you hope they would gain?

What kind of experiences did you imagine?

What values did you hope the game would reinforce?

On the next page, write a letter to your child, not about golf, but about who they are becoming.

This letter is not for today.

It's for years from now.

Golf will change.

Your child's swing will change.

Their goals will change.

Their relationship with the game will evolve.

What should not change is the foundation you've helped build.

A foundation of trust.

A foundation of safety.

A foundation of growth over fear.

Children raised on this foundation don't just succeed in golf.

They succeed in life.

A Parent's Promise

As you close this book, consider making one final commitment to your role within your child's golf experience.

I promise to protect the relationship first.

I promise to trust development over urgency.

I promise to let golf be a teacher, not a measure of worth.

Personalize this promise and write your own version on the next page.

Sign it.

This promise is not about perfection.

It's about intention.

Raising a lifelong champion doesn't mean raising a golfer who wins every weekend.

It means raising a person who stays curious, resilient, and connected, to themselves and to the game.

Golf will offer your child many lessons.

The greatest one they may learn is this:

They are enough, whether the putt drops or not.

And if that lesson takes hold, then regardless of where golf leads, you will have succeeded.

Not just as a golf parent.

But as a parent.

APPENDIX A

Quick Start Guide

THIS APPENDIX IS DESIGNED to help you begin immediately, without overthinking, overplanning, or overwhelming your child.

You do not need to read the entire book before taking action.

You do not need to change everything at once.

You simply need to set the tone.

That tone begins with one promise.

Day 1: The Foundation Promise

Before any clubs are swung, practices are scheduled, or tournaments are entered, establish the foundation of your child's golf journey.

This foundation is not technical.

It is relational.

Read the Parent's Promise aloud to your child.

The Parent's Promise

Read this aloud. Slowly. Without distraction.

Before we start this golf journey together, I need you to know something important.

You are my child first, always.

Golf is something you do, not who you are.

Whether you play well or struggle, whether you win or lose, whether you continue with golf or choose a different path someday, my love and support will never change.

I promise to be on your side, to support your effort, and to protect our relationship no matter what happens on the course.

That is my promise to you.

Parent Signature: ________________________

Date: ________________

Post this promise somewhere visible, on a wall, refrigerator, or inside a golf bag, where it can be seen regularly.

Week 1: Resetting the Environment

During the first week, focus on awareness rather than change.

- Observe how golf conversations typically happen
- Notice reactions after practice and competition
- Pay attention to emotional patterns, not outcomes

Do **not** correct everything at once.

Small awareness leads to lasting change.

Week 2: Simplifying Practice

Shift the goal of practice from "getting better" to "staying engaged."

- Shorter sessions are acceptable
- Curiosity matters more than repetition
- Games and challenges are encouraged

If enthusiasm increases, you're on the right track.

Week 3: Competition Reframed

Before the next competition:

- Remind your child that tournaments are information, not judgment
- Avoid setting outcome-based expectations
- Focus on effort, decisions, and response

After competition:

- Lead with connection
- Delay analysis unless your child initiates it

Week 4: Reflection and Adjustment

At the end of the first month:

- Reflect on emotional changes

- Notice shifts in confidence, engagement, and enjoyment
- Adjust expectations if needed

Progress is not measured by scores alone.

Final Reminder

You do not need to do everything perfectly.

Consistency matters more than intensity.

Presence matters more than instruction.

Relationship matters more than results.

This guide is not a checklist to complete.

It is a starting point.

APPENDIX B

Age-Based Development Guide

CHILDREN DO NOT DEVELOP at the same rate.

This is true physically, emotionally, cognitively, and socially. One of the biggest mistakes in junior golf is assuming that age alone determines readiness. Age provides a **general framework**, not a guarantee.

This guide is designed to help parents understand what is *developmentally appropriate* at different stages, not to create expectations, but to prevent unnecessary pressure.

Ages 5–7: Exploration and Play

At this stage, golf should feel like play.

Children are developing basic coordination, balance, and body awareness. Attention spans are short. Learning happens best through movement, imagination, and fun.

What to emphasize

- Enjoyment of the game
- Simple motion, not technique
- Basic contact and direction
- Games, challenges, and creativity

What to avoid

- Technical instruction
- Long practice sessions
- Scorekeeping or performance evaluation
- Formal competition pressure

Parent reminder

At this age, children are not "behind."

They are *beginning*.

If your child is smiling, curious, and asking to play again, development is happening.

Ages 8–10: Skill Discovery

This stage is marked by rapid learning and growing curiosity.

Children begin to understand cause and effect. They can follow simple instructions and enjoy structured challenges, especially when framed as games.

What to emphasize

- Variety in practice
- Shot experimentation
- Basic routines
- Introduction to friendly competition

What to avoid

- Over-coaching
- Constant correction

- Comparing progress to peers
- Attaching identity to scores

Parent reminder

Improvement may come quickly at this stage, but it is temporary and uneven.

Celebrate curiosity, not outcomes.

Ages 11–13: Transition and Change

This is one of the most misunderstood stages in junior golf.

Growth spurts, emotional shifts, and changing social dynamics all collide. Coordination often fluctuates. Confidence can dip unexpectedly.

What to emphasize

- Patience during inconsistency
- Emotional support
- Adaptability in practice

- Communication and listening

What to avoid

- Panicking over regression
- Increasing pressure to "fix" issues
- Expecting linear improvement
- Forcing competition volume

Parent reminder

Struggle during this phase is normal.

Regression is often a sign of reorganization, not failure.

Ages 14–16: Identity and Independence

Golf begins to mean more during this stage.

Children start forming identity. Motivation can fluctuate. Some become more committed; others question their involvement.

What to emphasize

- Ownership of goals
- Decision-making skills
- Mental and emotional regulation
- Balance with school and life

What to avoid

- Controlling schedules without input
- Defining worth through performance
- Ignoring emotional fatigue
- Over-specialization without rest

Parent reminder

This is a critical stage for autonomy.

Involvement without control strengthens motivation.

Ages 17–18+: Refinement and Direction

At this stage, golf becomes a choice.

Some players pursue higher-level competition. Others transition to recreational play or step away temporarily. Both paths are valid.

What to emphasize

- Self-reflection
- Process over outcome
- Life balance
- Transferable skills learned through golf

What to avoid

- Forcing continuation
- Guilt-based motivation
- Comparing paths to others
- Ignoring long-term well-being

Parent reminder

Success is not defined by how far golf goes, but by what it gives your child.

Final Perspective

Age-based guidelines are not rules.

They are **guardrails**, meant to protect children from adult urgency and misplaced expectations.

Development unfolds on its own schedule.

Your role is not to accelerate it.

Your role is to support it.

Appendix C

Practice Guidelines

Practice is where learning happens, but only when it is aligned with how children actually develop skills.

This guide is not a prescription. It is a set of principles designed to help parents recognize whether practice is helping or quietly hurting progress.

Purpose of Practice

Practice exists to:

- Build skill through experience
- Develop confidence through problem-solving
- Increase adaptability under changing

conditions

- Maintain enjoyment and curiosity

Practice is **not** meant to:

- Eliminate mistakes
- Perfect technique
- Impress others
- Replace competition

Length of Practice Sessions

Shorter, focused sessions are more effective than long, unfocused ones.

General guidelines:

- Younger children benefit from brief sessions with natural breaks
- Older children benefit from intentional segments rather than continuous hitting

- When attention fades, learning fades

If engagement drops, the session is complete, even if time remains.

Structure of Practice

Effective practice includes:

- A clear intention (what is being explored)
- Variety in tasks and targets
- Opportunity for adjustment and decision-making
- Periodic reflection

Rigid routines reduce learning over time.

Flexible structure supports adaptation.

Role of Repetition

Repetition is useful only when attention is present.

Mindless repetition:

- Builds habits without understanding
- Reduces feel
- Increases frustration

Intentional repetition:

- Reinforces awareness
- Supports confidence
- Improves transfer to the course

Quality always outweighs quantity.

Use of Games

Games are not a reward for good practice.

They *are* practice.

Games:

- Increase engagement
- Create emotional resilience
- Encourage adaptability
- Prepare children for competition

If practice never includes games, important skills are being missed.

Parent Involvement in Practice

Parents should:

- Observe more than instruct
- Encourage effort without directing outcomes
- Avoid real-time correction
- Allow children to explore solutions

Practice should feel safe, not evaluative.

Signs of Effective Practice

Practice is working when:

- Your child wants to return
- Focus is present
- Curiosity is visible
- Confidence slowly increases

Practice needs adjustment when:

- Sessions feel forced
- Frustration dominates
- Engagement drops consistently
- Enjoyment disappears

Final Reminder

Practice does not need to look impressive.

It needs to feel productive to the child.

When practice aligns with curiosity, learning accelerates.

Appendix D

Tournament Readiness Checklist**

Tournaments are not just tests of skill.

They test emotional readiness, adaptability, and response to pressure. This checklist is designed to help parents determine whether competition will *support* development, or strain it.

This is not about being "good enough."

It's about being ready to learn.

Emotional Readiness

Before entering competition, consider the following:

- Does your child recover reasonably well after

mistakes?

- Can they stay engaged even when things don't go their way?
- Do they show curiosity rather than fear around competition?
- Are emotional reactions manageable without adult intervention?

If emotions consistently overwhelm your child, more time is needed.

Motivational Readiness

Ask yourself:

- Does your child want to compete?
- Are they excited, or anxious?
- Do they understand *why* they are playing?

Competition should feel chosen, not assigned.

Practice Readiness

Before competing, your child should:

- Have practiced responding to different outcomes
- Be familiar with games and variability
- Understand basic routines
- Feel comfortable making decisions independently

Competition should not introduce stress your child has never experienced before.

Parental Readiness

Parents are part of the competitive environment.

Before tournaments, reflect on:

- Your expectations

- Your emotional investment
- Your likely reactions to struggle

If parents feel anxious, children will feel it too.

Environmental Readiness

Consider:

- Travel demands
- Cost
- Scheduling balance
- Recovery time between events
- School and social load

Competition should not crowd out the rest of childhood.

Post-Tournament Plan

Before competition begins, decide:

- How the car ride home will feel
- Whether analysis will be immediate or delayed
- How connection will be prioritized

Clarity reduces pressure.

Final Perspective

Readiness is not permanent.

A child may be ready one season and need a step back the next. Adjustments are not regressions.

They are responsiveness.

Appendix E

Post-Round Reflection Tools

What happens *after* a round matters as much as what happens during it.

Children don't just remember shots.

They remember emotions, reactions, and conversations.

They remember how it felt to finish.

This appendix is designed to help parents support learning **without turning reflection into evaluation**.

The Purpose of Post-Round Reflection

Post-round reflection should:

- Help children process experiences

- Reinforce learning without judgment
- Support emotional regulation
- Strengthen independence

Post-round reflection should **not**:

- Rehash mistakes repeatedly
- Assign blame
- Compare performance
- Determine worth or direction

Reflection is about understanding, not fixing.

Timing Matters

Immediately after a round:

- Emotions are still active
- Perspective is limited
- Analysis is rarely helpful

The best immediate response is:

- Connection
- Calm presence
- Neutral tone

Reflection is most effective **after emotions settle**.

Parent-Led Reflection (When Appropriate)

If your child is open to talking, keep reflection simple.

Helpful questions include:

- "What felt good out there today?"
- "What did you notice about how you responded?"
- "What did you learn about yourself?"

Avoid "why" questions early.

They often feel accusatory, even when well-intended.

Child-Led Reflection (Preferred)

The most powerful reflections are initiated by the child.

When children begin talking on their own:

- Listen more than you speak
- Resist correcting interpretations
- Validate effort and awareness

Silence is allowed.

Processing takes time.

Separating Outcome from Experience

Help your child distinguish:

- What happened (facts)
- How it felt (emotion)
- What was learned (insight)

Scores belong in the first category only.

Written Reflection Option

For children who prefer writing or drawing:

- Encourage brief notes
- Focus on feelings and responses
- Avoid score fixation

This is optional, not mandatory.

Red Flags to Watch For

Reflection may be harming learning if:

- Your child avoids talking altogether
- Conversations become tense
- Self-criticism increases

- Golf feels heavier afterward

When this happens, reduce reflection and increase space.

Final Reminder

The goal of reflection is not improvement by tomorrow.

It's understanding over time.

When reflection feels safe, learning sticks.

Appendix F

The Parent Promise Card

This promise is the foundation of everything in this book.

It is not about golf.

It is about relationship.

Before practices, tournaments, rankings, or goals, this promise comes first.

The Parent Promise

Read this aloud to your child.

I promise to love you and support you no matter how you play.

I promise that golf will never define who you are or how proud I am of you.

I promise to care more about your effort, your attitude, and your growth than your score.

I promise to protect our relationship before I protect results.

I promise to listen more than I instruct, and to support more than I correct.

I promise that whether you play great, struggle, or someday choose a different path, I am on your side, always.

Parent Signature: ______________________

Date: ________________

How to Use This Card

- Read it before the season begins
- Revisit it after difficult rounds
- Return to it when emotions rise
- Keep it visible as a reminder

This promise is not a rule.

It is a commitment.

Final Note

Children rarely remember every lesson.

They remember how they felt.

This promise shapes that feeling.

ACKNOWLEDGEMENTS

This book exists because of the countless families who shared their stories—both triumphs and struggles—with remarkable honesty and vulnerability.

Special thanks to:

- The young golfers who reminded me daily why joy matters most
- The parents who had the courage to change course when needed
- The coaches who prioritize development over winning
- The researchers whose work provides our foundation
- My family, for their patience during writing and wisdom throughout

To every parent reading this: Your willingness to examine and possibly change your approach takes tremendous courage. Your child is fortunate to have someone who cares enough to seek better ways.

May your journey be filled with more joy than you imagined possible.

A Final Word

If you take only one message from this book, let it be this:

Your child's relationship with golf will mirror your relationship with their golf journey. Choose joy, and they will too. Choose pressure, and they will feel it. Choose love over results, and they will play with freedom.

The game of golf offers profound gifts—integrity, resilience, patience, and joy. But these gifts can only be received with open hands, not grasping ones. Hold your child's golf journey lightly. Support without steering. Celebrate without comparing. Love without conditions.

Do this, and twenty years from now, you won't be looking at dusty trophies wondering where the time went. You'll be on the first tee with your adult child, sharing another round in a lifetime of rounds, grateful for every moment of the journey.

That's success. That's legacy. That's love. Play on!

About the Author

Father, Golf Coach, Educator,
Junior Development Leader

Joe DiChiara is a world-renowned golf coach with over two decades of experience coaching golfers of all levels—from beginners to major champions on the PGA and LPGA Tours. Recognized for his cutting-edge approach that blends biomechanics, motor learning science, and performance technology, Joe has earned a reputation as one of the most innovative minds in modern golf instruction.

Beyond his work with elite players, Joe is deeply committed to developing the next generation of golfers.

He has built and led nationally ranked junior golf programs, designed skill acquisition systems grounded in research, and mentored hundreds of young athletes through every stage of their golf journey. His programs emphasize not just swing mechanics, but also character development, competitive readiness, and long-term athletic growth.

Joe's impact on junior golf is matched by his leadership in golf education. He was the Co-Founder and Director of the International Preparatory Golf Academy in Bangkok, Thailand—now one of Asia's premier junior golf development programs. During his tenure, he coached and mentored numerous young athletes into U.S. college golf scholarships and guided two-time U.S. Women's Open Champion Yuka Saso.

Joe has also held executive positions as Director of Education with leading golf technology companies such as K-Motion, 4D Motion, and Sportsbox AI, where he helped bring advanced motion capture tools to coaches and athletes worldwide.

Currently, Joe resides in Phoenix, Arizona, where he serves as the Founder and Director of his golf academy as well as his online coaching programs. Whether on the range, in the lab, or guiding juniors toward college scholarships, Joe's mission remains the same: to make golf improvement accessible, personal, and transformative.

Joe would love to hear your story & can be reached at:
Joe@joedichiaragolf.com

www.ingramcontent.com/pod-product-compliance
Lightning Source LLC
LaVergne TN
LVHW020716110826
845149LV00012B/2284

9798994142233